ABUNDANT TRUTH INTERNATIONAL MINISTRIES

Kingdom Discipleship Series

The Dynamics of Discipleship

An Introductory Study of Discipleship and Service

Roderick Levi Evans

Published by Abundant Truth Publishing
P.O. Box 126 * Camden, NC 27921
Phone: 1-877-841-7209 * Fax: 1-877-841-7209
Web: www.abundantpublishing.net
Email: abundantpublishing@gmail.com

Printed U.S.A.

Front & Back Cover Designs by Abundant Truth Publishing
Image by Claudio Duart

> Abundant Truth Publishing is a ministry of Abundant Truth International Ministries. The primary mission of ATI Ministries is to equip the Body of Christ with tools necessary to defend and contend for the truth of the Christian faith. Jesus Christ came to bear witness of the truth and ATI Ministries is a modern-day extension of His commission (John 18:37).

The Dynamics of Discipleship: An Introductory Study of Discipleship and Service
©2025 Abundant Truth Publishing
All Rights Reserved

ISBN: 9781088238172

Contents

Introduction

Book 1 – The Development of the Discipleship   1

Introduction   3

Chapter 1 - The Process is Crucial   7

Our Lives are on the Menu   10
Remember Shadrach, Meshach and Abednego   12

Chapter 2 - The Ministry of Jesus   17

Jesus as Bread   20
The Church (His body) as Bread   24

Contents (cont.)

Chapter 3 - Understanding the Cleansing of the Process — 29
The Cleansing of Christ — 31
The Processing of Christ — 32

Chapter 4 – Understanding the Discipline of the Process — 39
The Control of Christ — 41
The Protection of Christ — 44

Chapter 5 - Final Thoughts on the Process — 49
The Disciple's Deliberation — 51

Book 2 - Keys to Ministry — 55
Introduction — 57

Contents (cont.)

Chapter 1 - Origin of Man   61
The Desire of God   65
The Destiny of Man   66

Chapter 2 - Obstinance of Man 73
The Standard of Adam   77
The Redemption of Mankind   79

Chapter 3 - Obedience of Man 85
The Cause of Christ   89
The Conformity of Man   91

Chapter 4 - Obstacles of Man 97
Submission   101
Spiritual Endeavors   104
Closing Thoughts   108

Contents (cont.)

Book 3 - Keys to the Promises of God   **113**

Introduction   115

Chapter 1: The Promise is Made   **121**

Forsaking the World   126
Ignoring the Circumstances   128

Chapter 2: The Promise is Delayed   **133**

It's Not Your Fault   135
It's God's Plan   137

Chapter 3: The Promise is Clarified   **143**

Change Self-Perception   148

Contents (cont.)

Change Approach to God   152

Chapter 4: The Promise is Fulfilled   **157**
God Keeps His Promise   162
Chapter 5: Your "Sarah" will have a Son   **165**
Wait on the Appointed Time Wait   170
Wait in Faith   171

Scripture References   **175**
The Promise of an Heir   177
Abraham and Sarah is Promised a Son   181

Book 4 – Walk in the Spirit   **187**
Introduction

Contents (cont.)

Section 1- The Spirit's In Involvement   **193**

Gods' Standard   195
Live By the Spirit   197
The Necessity of Discernment   199

Section 2- Lessons from the Parable of the Prodigal Son   **215**

The Attitude of the Faithful Son   219
The Attitude of Believers Today   221

Section 3 – Keys to Kingdom Conduct   **225**

Kingdom Character   227
Deny the Flesh   229
Live by the Spirit   231

Contents (cont.)

Obey the Word   233

Section 4 – Rewards of Kingdom 239
Conduct
Healing   242
Answered Prayer   243
Peace   245
Table of Contents (cont.)
Eternal Life   246

Bibliography   251

Introduction

Jesus called His followers disciples. A disciple is a convinced adherent of a school or individual who accepts and assists in spreading the doctrines of another. A Christian must not only believe on Jesus but be willing to share the faith of Jesus Christ. In order to do this, the believer has to not only understand his role as a disciple but know how to defend his beliefs.

The Kingdom Discipleship Series explores the biblical truths that should assist the believer in developing as a disciple of Christ. Not only will Christians grow in their walk with the Lord, but their understanding of foundational biblical truths will also expand.

In this publication

In this book, we will bring clarity to Christian discipleship and service. All in the Body of Christ are called first to discipleship and then to ministry and service in divers areas. The information present will give a foundation for the Christian disciple.

This publication is comprised of 4 distinct works:

1) The Development of the Disciple: The Preparation of the Christian for Ministry and Service

2) Keys to Ministry: Discovering the Foundation for Service and ministry in the Church

3) Keys to the Promises of God: Maintaining Faith While You Wait

4) Walk in the Spirit: Biblical Studies in Christian Conduct

It is our prayer that a greater understanding and appreciation for the prophetic gift and ministry will be achieved.

The Dynamics of Discipleship A Comprehensive Study of Discipleship and Service

-Book 1-
The Development of the Disciple

The Preparation of the Christian for Ministry and Service

(Potter's Wheel Study Series)

The Dynamics of Discipleship

A Comprehensive Study of Discipleship and Service

Introduction

Ministry and service in the kingdom of God is a privilege. God calls every member of the Body of Christ to serve for the benefit and welfare of the Body of Christ. However, we must remember that there are personal preparations that God requires for service.

The Potter's Wheel Study Series is designed to help believers recognize and apply the personal preparation that God implements for those called to minister and to serve. It is our prayer that the minister and the laymen will respond to God's personal preparations for ministry and service.

The Dynamics of Discipleship — A Comprehensive Study of Discipleship and Service

In this Publication

As a mother watches over her cuisine, as an artist is meticulous in preparing the work of art, and as a farmer watches carefully over the plantings, so the Lord watches over us with care.

The same level of care, caution, and concern a person uses in the preparation of a meal reflects God's care, caution, and concern for us. In this publication, learn how to recognize and submit to God's development of you as a disciple.

The Dynamics of Discipleship — A Comprehensive Study of Discipleship and Service

-Chapter 1-

The Process is Crucial

Understanding God's Preparation

Ministry Guides Series

The Dynamics of Discipleship

A Comprehensive Study of Discipleship and Service

How many of you remember when you were young and your mother or someone would be cooking something that you liked? Some of us would try to sneak in and peak at the food. Others of us would be more daring and try to get a taste.

However, disappointment would come when we would find that they would tell us it is not ready, and not to touch it or taste it. They sometimes would yell or smack our hands if we would go into what was being prepared.

Our Lives are on the Menu

This illustration was given so that you would understand how God watches over us as He prepares us to be shared with the world. As a mother watches over her cuisine, the Lord watches over us with care.

Baking and cooking is such an adequate analogy of how God prepares us to be strong and mature disciples. Also, it is an excellent pattern for how Christ prepares us for fruitful Christian service.

Before anything can be served, it has to be prepared. Some dishes are cold dishes. This reflects the times of isolation the Christian has to endure while God deals with their hearts by His Spirit.

Usually, times of acute loneliness are not always the work of individuals turning their backs on us, but a God ordained separation that we can commune with God without personal distractions.

Remember Shadrach, Meshach and Abednego

Other dishes have to be placed in extreme heat to be served. This demonstrates the numerous times of trials, tests, and temptations that can punctuate the Christian's life.

We oftentimes feel like we are experiencing fires similar to those that Shadrach, Meshach, and Abednego had to face.

Just as the fires did not consume them, but God sent His angel for their survival, so at the "hottest" time in our lives, God is only testing us, with the guarantee of victory in them because He will be with us during the worst times so that we will not be consumed.

The Dynamics of Discipleship

A Comprehensive Study of Discipleship and Service

Ministry Guides Series 14

Notes:

-Chapter 2-

The Ministry of Jesus

His Life as an Example for Today's Disciples

Jesus came as the Bread of heaven.

His disciples become bread also

when we come to know Him.

Our life and ministry can be comparable to a meal prepared for consumption. Even when Jesus spoke concerning His purpose, He referred to Himself as bread.

For the bread of God is he which cometh down from heaven, and giveth life unto the world. Then said they unto him, Lord, evermore give us this bread. And Jesus said unto them, I am the bread of life: he that cometh to me shall never hunger;

and he that believeth on me shall never thirst. (John 6:33-35)

Jesus as Bread

Jesus began teaching in Capernaum after feeding the five thousand. He presented them with the truth of who He was and that He was sent from the Father. He also challenged their doctrines by affirming that He was the Son of God, but also that they did not know God.

He that is of God heareth God's words: ye therefore hear them not, because ye are not of God. (John 8:47)

In addition, He claimed that except they drank His blood and ate His body, they could not have eternal life.

Then Jesus said unto them, Verily, verily, I say unto you, Except ye eat the flesh of the Son of man, and drink his blood, ye have no life in you. Whoso eateth my flesh, and drinketh my blood, hath eternal life; and I will raise him up at the last day. For my flesh is meat indeed, and my blood is drink indeed. He that eateth my flesh, and drinketh my blood, dwelleth in me, and I in him. As the living Father hath sent me, and I live by the Father: so he that eateth me, even he shall live by me. (John 6:53-57)

They were enraged. They thought of cannibalism which was an

abomination to any Jew. However, we know that Jesus spoke of His life and ministry. He was the word made flesh.

The scriptures declared that man shall not live by bread alone, but by the word that proceeds from God. Therefore, Christ came as living bread to be 'consumed' by those who believed. We know that Jesus' life was predestined by God. As a mother prepares a meal, so He was prepared to be served the world.

The foreshadowing of this truth was demonstrated in the miracles of feeding the multitudes. Jesus, only one man, served multitudes salvation.

The Church (His body) as Bread

Jesus came to meet the spiritual needs of the world, just as God gave Israel bread for their survival. Seeing that the Church is now His body, it bears the responsibility to still be the bread to a lost and dying world.

Jesus broke bread to demonstrate His suffering for the world. Likewise,

God will allow believers to be broken so that we can provide pure ministry and service to the world, which should ultimately result in many coming unto Him by faith.

His disciples are expected to do the same. The same level of care, caution, and concern that God used to prepare Christ is the same for a believer.

Notes:

The Dynamics of Discipleship — A Comprehensive Study of Discipleship and Service

-Chapter 3-

Understanding the Cleansing of the Process

Cleansing for Christian Life and Service

Christ will use various means and methods to prepare us for Christian life and service.

The Dynamics of Discipleship
A Comprehensive Study of Discipleship and Service

In section 1 we described how the preparation used to produce a meal reflects God's process in developing our lives and ministry.

The Cleansing of Christ

God, first, has to **cleanse** us and surrounding areas, as a mother cleans the food and surfaces to prepare a meal.

What areas does the Lord have to clean? He cleans areas such as ungodly family and friend relationships. In addition, habits and sins that are stunting our growth in Him. Finally, things in our lives that are unfruitful.

Now ye are clean through the word which I have spoken unto you. (John 15:3)

Then will I sprinkle clean water upon you, and ye shall be clean: from all your filthiness, and from all your idols, will I cleanse you. (Ezekiel 36:25)

The Processing of Christ

God puts us through **processing**

before He puts us on display. A mother has to chop, slice, dice, and strain. God does the same.

There is a process that God takes us through. The process is designed to push us into purpose. Oftentimes, He uses suffering in our lives to bring us into obedience. Even Jesus learned obedience through suffering,

Though he were a Son, yet learned he obedience by the things which he suffered. (Hebrews 5:8)

Therefore, God will shake and root up things in lives in the process, in order to produce substance in us.

At what instant I shall speak concerning a nation, and concerning a kingdom, to pluck up, and to pull down, and to destroy it. (Jeremiah 18:7)

He spoke through the prophet so Israel would know that He had control over their lives. The same is true for us. At any instant, God can allow trials to come if it pleases Him.

The Dynamics of Discipleship

A Comprehensive Study of Discipleship and Service

Notes:

The Dynamics of Discipleship

A Comprehensive Study of Discipleship and Service

-Chapter 4-

Understanding the Discipline of the Process

Discipline for Christian Life and Service

Christ will use numerous experiences to endure discipline, longevity, and fruitfulness in Christian's discipleship.

The Control of Christ

God **controls** the fire needed to prepare us. As a mother controls the temperature to make her meals, He adjusts the control so as not to damage us.

As with cooking, the temperature has to be set depending upon the dish. Therefore, when God allows the heat of trials, tests, and sufferings, we can have faith that all is under His control.

Beloved, think it not strange

concerning the fiery trial which is to try you, as though some strange thing happened unto you: But rejoice, inasmuch as ye are partakers of Christ's sufferings; that, when his glory shall be revealed, ye may be glad also with exceeding joy. (I Peter 4:12-13)

Just like a dish that is placed in the oven, it will seem as if we are left all alone. But remember, the heat is controlled.

The Dynamics of Discipleship

A Comprehensive Study of Discipleship and Service

Behold, I have refined thee, but not with silver; I have chosen thee in the furnace of affliction. For mine own sake, even for mine own sake, will I do it: for how should my name be polluted? And I will not give my glory unto another. (Isaiah 48:10-11)

God reminded Israel that He chose them in the furnace of affliction. As God prepares us for service, we will experience the 'oven' of despair and disappointment along with the heat of trials, tests, and sufferings. However, if we endure, we will be fruitful in power and character.

The Protection of Christ

God **protects** us from being touched too soon, as a mother protects her prepared dishes. As with cooking, there are external influences that could ruin a dish. When Jesus angered the Pharisees, they wanted to kill Him. However, they could not touch Him, because it was not time for

Him to be 'served.'

> *Then they sought to take him: but no man laid hands on him, because his hour was not yet come. (John 7:30)*

His enemies could not kill Him or hinder what God wanted to do through Him. The same applies to us. God will protect us and keep us during our times of preparation. He will finish what He starts in us.

> *Being confident of this very thing,*

that he which hath begun a good work in you will perform it until the day of Jesus Christ: (Philippians 1:6)

Notes:

-Chapter 5-

Final Thoughts on the Process

Considerations for Christian Life

and Service

The Dynamics of Discipleship

A Comprehensive Study of Discipleship and Service

The Christian must consider carefully what it means to be a disciple.

The Disciple's Deliberation

1. *Jesus was Bread from Heaven to be served to the multitudes for salvation.*

2. *God predestines us to be conformed to His image in order to serve us to the world.*

3. *Many do not last through the baking process and allow themselves to be damaged.*

4. *If food is not prepared properly, it will not taste good, could be dangerous to eat, and becomes*

of no use. The same is true for us if we do not submit to His process.

5. Your protection is in submitting to the process of the Lord. If you submit to God, you will exercise authority over the adversary.

6. If we submit to the process of God, nothing will be able to harm us, and we will be prepared for every adverse situation as Jesus was.

Notes:

The Dynamics of Discipleship A Comprehensive Study of Discipleship and Service

-Book 2-
Keys to Ministry
Discovering the Foundation for Service and ministry in the Church
(Christian Living Series)

The Dynamics of Discipleship — A Comprehensive Study of Discipleship and Service

Introduction

Peter told the believers that they were *stewards* of the manifold grace of God. This means that every follower of Christ has the responsibility to grow and develop in their God-given gifts. In addition, they are to be faithful in ministering to others.

The Kingdom Stewards Series was created to help believers understand their gifts and ministries. It is designed to bring clarity to the purpose and functions of spiritual gifts and ministries. It is our prayer that believers will grow in the recognition, acceptance, and operation of the gifts of God.

The Dynamics of Discipleship — A Comprehensive Study of Discipleship and Service

In this publication:

God's mandate for ministry in the kingdom begins with character. God gives us the authority and ability to minister to help others mature and grow in Him.

Ministry brings mankind back to God's original plan for them. His original plan was to have sons and daughters. However, man fell through disobedience and God had to provide another way for man to be conformed to His likeness and image.

In this publication, we will examine man's origin, man's obstinance, man's obedience, and man's obstacles to engaging in fruitful ministry and service. It is with this understanding that we can form the proper foundation to comprehend God's mandate for ministry.

The Dynamics of Discipleship

A Comprehensive Study of Discipleship and Service

-Chapter 1-

Origin of Man

The Dynamics of Discipleship

A Comprehensive Study of Discipleship and Service

And God said, Let us make man in our image, after our likeness: and let them have dominion over the fish of the sea, and over the fowl of the air, and over the cattle, and over all the earth, and over every creeping thing that creepeth upon the earth. (Genesis 1:26)

In the beginning, God plainly stated His purpose for creating man.

The Desire of God

He wanted man to have His likeness and image and have dominion and authority over all that He created.

> *And God said, Let us make man in our image, after our likeness: and let them have dominion over the fish of the sea, and over the*

fowl of the air, and over the cattle, and over all the earth, and over every creeping thing that creepeth upon the earth. (Genesis 1:26)

God's intent was for man to be like Him. When Adam was created, he was made in express image of God.

The Destiny of Man

God's intent has not changed. Therefore, when Adam failed, God sent the last Adam who would bring man back into the presence of God and fulfill the plan of creation: have man in God's likeness and image. We know that Christ came in the image of God. He states,

> *Jesus saith unto him, have I been so long time with you, and yet hast thou not known me, Philip? He that hath seen me hath seen the Father; and how sayest thou then, Shew us the*

Father? (John 14:9)

Jesus came to redeem man. His life is our example. He told Philip that if they had seen Him, they had seen the Father.

In the Garden, God created man like Himself and gave him a charge. He was to have dominion over all that was in the earth. Today, we find that creation rebels against man.

In addition, we find that though man was destined to walk in dominion, he walks in bondage to many influences. Therefore, God places the ability to minister in man to facilitate deliverance.

Notes:

-Chapter 2-

Obstinance of Man

The Dynamics of Discipleship

A Comprehensive Study of Discipleship and Service

For thou art an holy people unto the Lord thy God: the Lord thy God hath chosen thee to be a special people unto himself, above all people that are upon the face of the earth. (Deuteronomy 7:6)

God created man in all righteousness. However, we find that man was corrupted through disobedience. This resulted in generations of people who walked in disobedience and lived lives that were void of purpose and communion with God.

The Standard of Adam

That same Adam, who was to be the standard for all creation after him, disobeyed God.

And unto Adam he said, Because thou hast hearkened unto the voice of thy wife, and hast eaten of the tree, of which I commanded thee, saying, Thou shalt not eat of it: cursed is the ground for thy sake; in sorrow shalt thou eat of it all the days of thy life. (Genesis 3:17)

Man's fall resulted in a curse, whereby all that followed were affected. Men and women born in the earth became vulnerable to the trappings of sin and evil. Though man fell, God's plan and purpose for creating him never changed.

The Redemption of Mankind

Consequently, man's corruption needed a remedy. Therefore, God chose Israel to be His light in the earth. Through their obedience to God, all the nations of the earth would turn to God and be as He originally ordained.

For thou art an holy people unto the Lord thy God: the Lord thy God hath chosen thee to be a special people unto himself, above all people that are upon the face of the earth. (Deuteronomy 7:6)

Though they were to be a light to the Gentiles as God's chosen people, they continually rebelled against God. Therefore, God had to intervene again for the salvation of man. Even though they failed, God's original plan for man to be made in His image remained.

The Dynamics of Discipleship

A Comprehensive Study of Discipleship and Service

Ministry Guides Series

Notes:

The Dynamics of Discipleship
A Comprehensive Study of Discipleship and Service

-Chapter 3-
Obedience of Man

For whom he did foreknow, he also did predestinate to be conformed to the image of his Son, that he might be the firstborn among many brethren. (Romans 8:30)

The Dynamics of Discipleship

A Comprehensive Study of Discipleship and Service

God established the New Covenant upon the person and work of Christ. Because of man's corruption, God had to give men the ability to be conformed to His image and likeness.

The Cause of Christ

Christ came in the likeness of sinful flesh in order to deliver men from the bondage of sin.

For what the law could not do, in that it was weak through the flesh, God sending his own

Son in the likeness of sinful flesh, and for sin, condemned sin in the flesh: That the righteousness of the law might be fulfilled in us, who walk not after the flesh, but after the Spirit. (Romans 8:3-4)

The above scripture states that the result of His coming was that the righteousness of the law (God's standard for man) could be fulfilled or completed in men. The indwelling presence of the Spirit gives men the ability to fulfill the predestined will of God.

> *For whom he did foreknow, he also did predestinate to be conformed to the image of his Son, that he might be the firstborn among many brethren. (Romans 8:30)*

The Conformity of Man

The will of God is for men and women to be conformed to the image of Jesus Christ. He places individuals in ministry to perform this task.

When Paul listed the ministry offices as recorded in Ephesians 4, he states that their purpose is to cause the Church to come into the fullness of Christ's personality, not just His power.

> *His intention was the perfecting and the full equipping of the saints (His consecrated people), [that they should do] the work of*

the ministering toward building up Christ's body (the Church), [that if might develop] until we attain oneness in the faith and in the comprehension of the full and accurate knowledge of the Son of God; that [we might arrive] at really mature manhood – standard height of Christ's own perfection – the measure of the stature of the fullness of the Christ, and the completeness found in Him. (Ephesians 4:12-13 Amplified)

God intended for ministers to develop mature believers who reflect the nature of Christ. Ministry and gifts are given to help men conform to the image of God. Our gifts are to be used for this intent. We must remember that all ministry points to Christ, not ourselves.

Notes:

-Chapter 4-

Obstacles of Man

The Dynamics of Discipleship

A Comprehensive Study of Discipleship and Service

The Dynamics of Discipleship A Comprehensive Study of Discipleship and Service

The sheep that are My own hear and to My voice, and I know them and they follow Me. (John 10:27 Amplified)

The Dynamics of Discipleship

A Comprehensive Study of Discipleship and Service

After we have received Christ in our lives, one of the main obstacles that faces Vus is submission to ministry. If we cannot meet this challenge, we will fail before we get started.

Submission

Ministry does not begin with preaching a sermon, laying hands, prophesying, or praying. Ministry begins in us as we submit to the ministry of the Spirit.

Before we can minister, we first must receive ministry. The ministry of the Spirit is designed to make us like Christ. Without allowing the Spirit to minister to us, we will not be effective in ministry.

The question remains, "How do Spirit?" We submit to His ministry in two ways. First, we submit to Him by following the leading of His indwelling presence.

The Spirit of God comes to lead

and guide us into all truth. He not only leads us into truth concerning doctrine, but also into the truth about our personal weaknesses and hindrances.

Without submitting to His voice in our personal relationship with Him, it will be almost impossible to follow His voice in a ministry setting.

To follow His inner leading is not as difficult as some have made it. Jesus said that His sheep hears (knows) His voice.

> *The sheep that are My own hear and to My voice, and I know them and they follow Me. (John 10:27 Amplified)*

Spiritual Endeavors

Consistent prayer and study of the Word help the believer to know the voice of the Holy Spirit. When we are able to recognize His voice, we then have to follow His directives.

The second way we submit to the Holy Spirit is by following His instructions through others.

The Holy Spirit not only speaks to us personally, but He speaks to us through others. The Spirit of God releases gifts and ministries upon members of the Body of Christ for its edification.

But to each one is given the manifestation of the (Holy) Spirit – that is, the evidence, the spiritual illumination of the Spirit – for good and profit. (I Corinthians 12:7 Amplified)

We have to receive the gifts that God has placed in others for our benefit. If we learn to receive ministry, others will receive ministry from us. This is the beginning of ministry.

The challenge then remains for us to consistently receive ministry, which prepares us to minister. We receive ministry to develop His nature. When we are like Him, we will do His works.

God, who at sundry times and in divers manners spake in time past unto the fathers by the prophets, Hath in these last days spoken unto us by his Son, whom he hath appointed heir of all things, by whom also he made the worlds. (Hebrews 1:1-2)

The writer of Hebrews says that

in these last days God speaks to us through His Son. When we are like the Son, God can speak through us. He can then use us.

The character of Christ produces kingdom ministry. Without His nature, the proper foundation for ministry in the kingdom is not laid.

Closing Thoughts for the Kingdom Mandate for Ministry

1)   From the beginning, God's plan was to have sons and daughters.

2) Therefore, the Spirit of God comes to help us reflect His very nature and character.

3) If we possess His nature, we will do His works.

4) When we become like Christ, we will be able to do the greater works that He spoke of.

5) We must remember that before we can minister effectively, we must submit to ministry.

6) The ministry of the Spirit will

come from His inner voice and through others.

7) The Lord does all of this so that men can be conformed to Christ's image.

8) There is no other foundation for ministry except to be like God.

For a full examination of God's purpose for ministry, please see my book, "He Gave Gifts Unto Men: God's Mandate for Ministry in the Kingdom."

Notes:

The Dynamics of Discipleship — A Comprehensive Study of Discipleship and Service

-Book 3-

Keys to the Promises of God

Maintaining Faith While You Wait

(Abundant Truth International's Inspirational Series)

Introduction

The Christian life is simple and complex simultaneously. Its simplicity rests upon one truth: Jesus Christ is the Son of God and that faith in Him results in man's salvation. However, to live a fruitful Christian life comes from navigating through the complexities of life.

The Abundant Truth Inspirational Series was developed to aid the Christian in handling the difficulties that come with the Christian experience.

The Dynamics of Discipleship — A Comprehensive Study of Discipleship and Service

In this Publication

Do you keep promises that you make? How many times in life have we been disappointed because someone made us a promise and did not keep it?

We know that God is not like man. Whatever He says He is going to do, it shall be done. Whatever He has promised in the scriptures will surely be manifested in your life.

In light of this truth, many still have felt as if the Lord had forgotten them and begun to doubt the promises that He made to them. However, the Lord is going to perform His word.

In the biblical account of the patriarch Abraham, we find that God made him a promise. He told Abraham that he would have a son. However, he had to wait.

After some time had passed, Sarah did not conceive, and Abraham fathered a son by his handmaiden, Hagar. However, we discover that this was not the child of promise.

After more years had passed, we discover that God performed His word to Abraham and Sarah did have a son. From this story, we shall explore some valuable truths that will help us stand as we **wait** to possess the promise.

In the publication, we will look closely at the biblical account of God's promise to Abraham. From this, will discover truth to help Christians today to maintain faith as we wait on the promises of God.

-Chapter 1-

The Promise is Made

The Dynamics of Discipleship

A Comprehensive Study of Discipleship and Service

And, behold, the word of the Lord came unto him, saying, This shall not be thine heir; but he that shall come forth out of thine own bowels shall be thine heir. (Genesis 15:4)

The Dynamics of Discipleship

A Comprehensive Study of Discipleship and Service

Ministry Guides Series

After Abram (Abraham) returns from battle and gives tithes to Melchizedek, the Lord appears to him in a vision.

After these things the word of the Lord came unto Abram in a vision, saying, Fear not, Abram: I am thy shield, and thy exceeding great reward. And Abram said, Lord God, what wilt thou give me, seeing I go childless, and the stewar of my house is this Eliezer of Damascus? And Abram said, Behold, to me thou hast given no seed: and, lo, one born in my house is mine heir. (Genesis 15:1-3)

Abram asks the Lord that if you are my shield and exceeding great reward, then why have I not had a son.

Forsaking the World

Abram had left everything familiar to him to follow the Lord. However, the Lord did not bless him with a child. Does his question to the Lord sound like us today?

We have left the world and the lusts therein only to find that we have not received all that we think the Lord should give us. This was the mindset of Abram. Following in the passage, we find that God speaks to Abram and tells him that he would have the son that he has desired.

And, behold, the word of the Lord came unto him, saying, This shall not be thine heir; but he that shall come forth out of thine own bowels shall be thine heir. (Genesis 15:4)

Ignoring the Circumstances

God spoke this to him in spite of the facts:

1. ***He was old.***

2. ***Sarai, his wife, was old.***

3. ***Sarai was barren.***

We discover, in spite of the obstacles, that Abram believed the Lord.

And he believed in the Lord;

and he counted it to him for righteousness. (Genesis 15:6)

We, too, must stand on the promises of God. God made him a promise in the most unfavorable conditions. We must understand that our present circumstances and conditions do not negate or hinder the promises of God from coming to pass in our lives.

If God has made you a promise or you are believing God for something by faith – continue to believe. If Abram could believe against the odds, so can we.

Personal Thoughts:

The Dynamics of Discipleship
A Comprehensive Study of Discipleship and Service

-Chapter 2-

The Promise is Delayed

The Dynamics of Discipleship

A Comprehensive Study of Discipleship and Service

When we think of the something being delayed, it is often attributed to some outside influence. However, the plan of God cannot be delayed except by God himself.

It's Not Your Fault

Do not think that you have done something wrong or someone else is hindering your blessing or promise from coming to pass. Whatever the Lord has for you, it is for you.

In our story, God did not bring the promise to pass immediately. We find that because of this, Sarai tells Abram to take her handmaid and have an heir by her.

And Sarai said unto Abram, Behold now, the Lord hath restrained me from bearing: I pray thee, go in unto my maid; it may be that I may obtain children by her. And Abram hearkened to the voice of Sarai. (Genesis 16:2)

This was **not** because they did not believe God.

He staggered not at the promise of God through unbelief; but was strong in faith, giving glory to God. (Romans 4:20)

It's God's Plan

For in God's promise to Abram, He had made no mention of Sarai. He told Abram from ***his*** own bowels would an heir come. Since the customs of the day allowed such a practice, Abram went into Hagar and she conceived and brought forth a son, calling him Ishmael.

And Hagar bare Abram a son: and Abram called his son's name, which Hagar bare, Ishmael. (Genesis 16:15)

However, we discover that this was not the fulfillment of the promise. How many times did it seem you were close to walking in what the Lord had promised, only to discover that it was not His will?

Oftentimes, we like Abram, produce "Ishmael" in our lives and we think it is the promise. This is why many are disappointed and discouraged.

When they thought God's promise was coming to pass and it was not received, rather than standing on the promise, they began to doubt that God had ever spoken to them.

We cannot doubt God's promise because of apparent delays and setbacks. His word to us will come to pass.

The Dynamics of Discipleship

A Comprehensive Study of Discipleship and Service

Personal Thoughts:

The Dynamics of Discipleship

A Comprehensive Study of Discipleship and Service

-Chapter 3-

The Promise is Clarified

The Dynamics of Discipleship

A Comprehensive Study of Discipleship and Service

And when Abram was ninety years old and nine, the Lord appeared to Abram, and said unto him, I am the Almighty God; walk before me, and be thou perfect. (Genesis 17:1)

The Dynamics of Discipleship

A Comprehensive Study of Discipleship and Service

Abram thought he was on his way. Hagar gave him a son who would be his heir. However, the Lord appears to him almost 13 years after the initial promise and gives Abram clarity.

> *And when Abram was ninety years old and nine, the Lord appeared to Abram, and said unto him, I am the Almighty God; walk before me, and be thou perfect. (Genesis 17:1)*

Change Self-Perception

The first thing God does is change his name to Abraham and give him the sign of circumcision.

Neither shall thy name any more be called Abram, but thy name shall be Abraham; for a father of many nations have I made thee. (Genesis 17:5)

Next, God tells Abraham to change his wife's name. In addition, God brings further clarity to the word originally spoken to Abraham. He would have a son, but it would be by his barren and old wife. Abraham was shocked and he laughed.

And God said unto Abraham, As for Sarai thy wife, thou shalt not call her name Sarai, but Sarah shall her name be. And I will bless her, and give thee a son also of her: yea, I will bless her, and she shall be a mother of nations; kings of people shall be of her. (Genesis 17:15 16)

He even pleaded with the Lord

for Ishmael. He wanted him to be his heir. However, the Lord would not hear it.

> Then Abraham fell upon his face, and laughed, and said in his heart, Shall a child be born unto him that is an hundred years old? and shall Sarah, that is ninety years old, bear? And Abraham said unto God, O that Ishmael might live before thee! And God said, Sarah thy wife shall bear thee a son indeed; and thou shalt

call his name Isaac: and I will establish my covenant with him for an everlasting covenant, and with his seed after him. (Genesis 17:17- 19)

This is where many believers miss the Lord. We, like Abraham, did not go back to the Lord with follow up questions after the promise is made.

This is the reason many people suffer unnecessary setbacks as they move toward the promises of God. They did not get clarity in the promise.

Change Approach to God

Since God had made mention Only of Abraham years earlier, Abraham did not ask God by whom he would have a child. We can suggest that he assumed it would be by someone other than his wife.

Because he asked no questions, he had to now deal with the fact that the son (from Hagar) whom he thought would be his heir was rejected by God.

In addition, he had to stand in

faith again as God now mentioned his heir coming from his old, barren wife. Paul tells us that after his dialogue with the Lord, he believed the Lord for it by faith.

> *And being not weak in faith, he considered not his own body now dead, when he was about an hundred years old, neither yet the deadness of Sarah's womb. (Romans 4:19)*

Some of you reading this have left off believing God for His promises because of delays and setbacks. It is time now for you to return to the Lord and ask for clarity regarding His promise. Some of your efforts have been fruitless because you have been going in unto Hagar and not Sarah.

Personal Thoughts:

-Chapter 4-

The Promise is Fulfilled

The Dynamics of Discipleship A Comprehensive Study of Discipleship and Service

And Abraham called the name of his son that was born unto him, whom Sarah bare to him, Isaac.

God fulfills His promise to Abraham. Sarah conceives and brings forth Isaac.

And the Lord visited Sarah as he had said, and the Lord did unto Sarah as he had spoken. For Sarah conceived, and bare Abraham a son in his old age, at the set time of which God had spoken to him. And Abraham called the name of his son that was born unto him, whom Sarah bare to him, Isaac. (Genesis 21:1-3)

God Keeps His Promise

The word of the Lord came to pass in a way that Abraham and Sarah did not think it would. In addition, the son was called Isaac, meaning "laughter."

This demonstrates to us that when God brings forth his promise in your life, you will have joy and laughter.

Personal Thoughts:

_____

_____

_____

_____

_____

_____

_____

_____

The Dynamics of Discipleship
A Comprehensive Study of Discipleship and Service

-Chapter 5-

Your "Sarah" will have a Son

The Dynamics of Discipleship
A Comprehensive Study of Discipleship and Service

God wants you to try again. After the Lord made his promise plain to Abraham, the only thing he had to do was to go in unto Sarah again.

Many of you have tried to wait and walk in the promise and plan of God your lives without major results.

Therefore, (like Abraham going into Hagar), your attention was still on the promise, but diverted to areas that seemed to be more productive.

Abraham did not realize that the woman he had gone into for years, without producing any fruit would be the one that would give him an heir.

Wait on the Appointed Time

This demonstrates to us that God's promise to us is always with us, just waiting until the appointed time to produce fruit. The very one that never gave him a son, became the vessel of his promise.

This shows us that the areas in our lives and ministries that have not been very productive will bring forth fruit, if we turn our attention from "Hagar and Ishmael" and focus again on "Sarah."

God wants you to try again. After the Lord made his promise plain to Abraham, the only thing he had to do was to go in unto Sarah again.

Wait in Faith

Many have given up on their ministries growing, family members receiving salvation, and even their bodies being healed. They have prayed, fasted, claimed, and believed and no results were found. However, walk in the faith of Abraham and go in again unto "Sarah."

Believe God again for growth in your ministry, present the gospel again unto unsaved family members, pray and believe God again for your healing.

For whatever your "Sarah" is, she will conceive and bring forth your "Isaac." This is the reward of the Art of Waiting.

Personal Thoughts:

The Dynamics of Discipleship

A Comprehensive Study of Discipleship and Service

-Appendix-

Scripture References

The Dynamics of Discipleship

A Comprehensive Study of Discipleship and Service

The Dynamics of Discipleship — A Comprehensive Study of Discipleship and Service

The Promise of an Heir
Genesis 15:1-7

1After these things the word of the LORD came unto Abram in a vision, saying, Fear not, Abram: I am thy shield, and thy exceeding great reward.

2And Abram said, Lord GOD, what wilt thou give me, seeing I go childless, and the steward of my house is this Eliezer of Damascus?

3And Abram said, Behold, to me thou hast given no seed: and, lo, one born in my house is mine heir.

4And, behold, the word of the LORD came unto him, saying, This shall not be thine heir; but he that shall come forth out of thine own bowels shall be thine heir.

5And he brought him forth abroad, and said, Look now toward heaven, and tell the stars, if thou be able to number them: and he said unto him, So shall thy seed be.

6And he believed in the LORD; and he counted it to him for righteousness.

7And he said unto him, I am the LORD that brought thee out of Ur of the Chaldees, to give thee this land to inherit it.

The Dynamics of Discipleship
A Comprehensive Study of Discipleship and Service

Abraham Is Promised a Son
Genesis 18:1-18

1 The Lord showed Himself to Abraham by the oak trees of Mamre, as he sat at the tent door in the heat of the day. 2 Abraham looked up and saw three men standing in front of him. When he saw them, he ran from the tent door to meet them. He put his face to the ground 3 and said, "My lord, if I have found favor in your eyes, please do not pass by your servant. 4

Let us have a little water brought to wash your feet. Rest yourselves under the tree. 5 And I will get a piece of bread so you may eat and get strength. After that you may go on your way, since you have come to your servant."

The men said, "Do as you have said." 6 So Abraham ran into the tent to Sarah, and said, "Hurry and get three pails of fine flour, mix it well, and make bread." 7 Then Abraham ran to the cattle and took out a young and good calf. He gave it to the servant to make it ready in a hurry. 8 He took milk and cheese and the meat which he had made ready, and set it in front of them. He stood by them under the tree while they ate.

9 Then they said to him, "Where is your wife Sarah?" And he said, "There in the tent." 10 The Lord said, "I will be sure to return to you at this time next year. And your wife Sarah will have a son." Sarah was listening at the tent door behind him. 11 Now Abraham

and Sarah were old. They had lived many years. The way of women had stopped for Sarah. 12 So Sarah laughed to herself, saying, "Will I have this joy after my husband and I have grown old?" 13 Then the Lord said to Abraham, "Why did Sarah laugh and say, 'How can I give birth to a child when I am so old?' 14 Is anything too hard for the Lord? I will return to you at this time next year, and Sarah will have a son." 15 But Sarah said, "I did not laugh," because she was afraid.

The Dynamics of Discipleship

A Comprehensive Study of Discipleship and Service

And He said, "No, but you did laugh."

The Dynamics of Discipleship

A Comprehensive Study of Discipleship and Service

The Dynamics of Discipleship — A Comprehensive Study of Discipleship and Service

-Book 4-

Walk in the Spirit

Biblical Studies in Christian Conduct

(Kingdom Citizens Series)

The Dynamics of Discipleship

A Comprehensive Study of Discipleship and Service

The Dynamics of Discipleship — A Comprehensive Study of Discipleship and Service

Introduction

Jesus told the disciples that He would give us the keys to the Kingdom. We know that He spoke of authority and access. The Kingdom Citizens series is designed to help believers live daily as followers of Christ.

Kingdom Citizens gives brief and vital information teaching Christians how to live under God's rule in a world that is opposed to Christ. It is our prayer that you will be blessed by the materials presented. Jesus said that it is our Father's good pleasure to give us the Kingdom.

The Dynamics of Discipleship

A Comprehensive Study of Discipleship and Service

In this Issue:

God has a standard of living that we, as believers, must live by. However, we must remember that our good works and acts must be a product of Christ's character being formed in us. In this publication, we will examine the proper conduct for the Christian.

Ministry Guides Series

The Dynamics of Discipleship

A Comprehensive Study of Discipleship and Service

The Dynamics of Discipleship

A Comprehensive Study of Discipleship and Service

-Section 1-

The Spirit's Involvement

The Dynamics of Discipleship

A Comprehensive Study of Discipleship and Service

All nations, provinces, countries, towns, cities, and territories have laws that govern them. They set laws as standards of conduct. They are in place to prohibit citizens from engaging in unlawful acts. The same is true in the Kingdom of God.

God's Standard

God has a standard of living that we, as believers, must live by. However, we must remember that our good works and acts must be a product of Christ's character being formed in us.

Because of their bad character traits, Christ condemned the Pharisees' good works. Our good works will also be nothing if the nature of Christ is not in us.

After the nature of Christ is in us, we must live according to His standards. We must live by the Spirit and not by the flesh.

Paul informs the believers at Galatia that if they would live by the Spirit, they would be able to control the flesh.

Live by the Spirit

This same rule applies to us today. To have Kingdom Conduct, we also have to live by the Spirit. It must be adhered to if we want to have the proper conduct.

How can we live by and obey the Spirit of God? How can we walk in the Spirit? We are instructed through the Word and by ministers to walk in the Spirit. It sounds good, but many are unsure of how to do it.

First, we must acknowledge and recognize the presence of the Holy Spirit in us. Then, we must respond to His leading and allow Him to control and guide our everyday actions.

But I say, "Walk and live habitually in the (Holy) Spirit – responsive to and controlled by the Spirit; then you will certainly not gratify the cravings and desires of the flesh – of human nature without God." (Galatians 5:16 Amplified)

When we live by the Spirit, we will find ourselves not falling into the same snares of our flesh and of the enemy. In order to have conduct fitting for the Kingdom, we must overcome the flesh.

Some do not know how to overcome the flesh. Others believe that all evil thoughts and actions are from demonic spirits.

The Necessity of Discernment

Because of certain teachings, we blame our fleshly desires on demonic activity rather than face them. In my book, The World, The Flesh, and The Devil, I discussed how to recognize the difference. Here is an excerpt:

"With the discovery of the existence of demons and the reality of spiritual warfare, believers today continue to place the blame for their desire to sin on the devil.

Believers have become so "spirit conscience" that they fail to realize that what they are calling a spirit is actually a characteristic of the flesh.

Because of this, believers fail to crucify the flesh and mortify its deeds. If someone is upset, it is said, "He has a spirit of anger."

If someone is full of pride, it is said, "He has a spirit of pride." In addition, if someone operates in lust, it is said, "He has a spirit of lust." Yet, the scriptures call all of these characterize deeds of the flesh.

Therefore, when sinful desires manifest in the flesh, the believer does not deal with his flesh, but rather places the blame on a "spirit." The believer is deceived. He will inevitably lead a defeated life because he will feel something beyond his control causes his sinful desires. He is, in actuality, fighting with an imaginary enemy. Paul tells us:

> *I therefore so run, not as uncertainly; so fight I, not as one that beateth the air. (I Corinthians 9:26)*

When the believer cannot a demonic spirit, he is running

uncertainly and fighting as one beating the air. It is important to note that before one can deal with the flesh, he must first be able to discern *what is flesh* and *what is a spirit.*

Distinguishing between flesh and spirit is simpler than what believers have been traditionally taught. Believers have been exposed to numerous teachings concerning the spiritual realm and demons.

Many have taught that Christians cannot have demons, while others believe that it is possible. They have been taught that demons are not real and that they are real. The list goes on and on.

In spite of all of these teachings, believers continue to struggle in their flesh on a daily basis. To simplify the subject of what is flesh and what is spirit, one must only look to the Word. Jesus also addressed the subject by saying:

When the unclean spirit is gone out of a man, he walketh through dry places, seeking rest; and finding none, he saith, I will return unto my house whence I came out. And when he cometh, he findeth it swept and garnished. Then goeth he, and taketh to him seven other spirits more wicked than himself; and they enter in, and dwell there: and the last state of that man is worse than the first. (Luke 11:24-26)

Jesus says that once an unclean spirit leaves out of a man, it looks for a place to rest. If it cannot find a new home, it will return to the man it came out of. Once back, it finds the man (house) empty and clean. We must be wise. If we do not fill our "house" with Christ and the Word after we are delivered from bondage, the enemy may be able to put us back into bondage.

The enemy has no more control over a believer than what the believer gives him. When an individual is converted, the power and control of sin is broken in his life.

Still, many new converts are neither strong nor knowledgeable enough to maintain freedom in every area of their lives.

Does this mean that spirits will be in them? Of course not! The principle set forth in this scripture is that a spirit may be present when there is an area of weakness in the flesh, which is not submitted to Christ.

Therefore, to be able to distinguish between what is flesh and spirit is simple. Again, wherever there is a weakness, the potential for a spirit to operate there is present. We must realize also that once the weak area is overcome, the door to the enemy is closed.

We must learn to close every door to the enemy. If we deal with our sinful desires, the concern with spirits will decrease and we can focus wholly on our personal walk with God.

The goal is not to necessarily fight the enemy or temptation, but to draw closer to God." **(Excerpt from The World, The Flesh, and The Devil, pgs. 23-25)**

Galatians 5:19-20 gives us a list of some of the attributes of the flesh. They are as follows: sexual immorality, impurity, and debauchery, idolatry and witchcraft, hatred, discord, jealousy, fits of rage, selfish ambition, dissension, factions and envy, drunkenness, and orgies (NIV).

We must understand that if we

are exhibiting any of these traits in our lifestyle, our conduct will not be suitable for Kingdom living. We must not be afraid to say these things are in our flesh.

We must be careful not to refer to these "workings of the flesh" as spirits, when they are not. The works of the flesh must be crucified.

In our publication, "Let This Mind Be In You," we discussed character. It is understood that our conduct is a direct reflection of our character.

Therefore, if you develop character, the right conduct is soon to follow. Conversely, the reverse of this may not work in the same manner. We have numerous examples in the Bible of individuals who had the right conduct, but character was nonexistent.

Kingdom Notes:

The Dynamics of Discipleship

A Comprehensive Study of Discipleship and Service

-Section 2-

Lessons from the Parable of the Prodigal Son

The Dynamics of Discipleship
A Comprehensive Study of Discipleship and Service

Through this parable, we are given an illustration of how one can have the right conduct, but wrong character.

Now his elder son was in the field: and as he came and drew nigh to the house, he heard musick and dancing. And he called one of the servants, and asked what these things meant. And he said unto him, Thy brother is come; and thy father hath killed the fatted calf, because he hath received him safe and sound. And he was angry, and would not go in: therefore came his father out, and entreated him. And he answering said to his father, Lo, these many years do I serve thee, neither transgressed I at any time thy commandment: and yet thou never gavest me a kid, that I might make merry with my friends: But as soon as this thy son was come, which hath devoured thy living with harlots, thou hast killed for him the fatted calf. And he said unto him, Son, thou art ever with me, and all that I have is thine. It was meet that we should make merry, and be glad: for this thy brother was dead, and is alive again; and was lost, and is found. (Luke 15:25-32)

The Attitude of the Faithful Son

The son that remained home possessed the right conduct, but had no character. He stayed home. He obeyed his father. He worked. He did not wrongfully use any of his father's possessions, though he was an heir. However, we also find that his attitude was bad.

He was not happy when he discovered that his brother returned home. He did not even attend the festivities. He defamed his brother to his father. He wanted to appear more righteous than his brother. All of this sprang up from his character and the lack thereof. His example should serve as a warning to us.

The Attitude of Believers Today

There are believers today who are faithful to the Church and its activities. They serve on many boards and oftentimes, they are ministers. However, some of us have experienced the wrath of some of these individuals.

They continued to work for the Lord but failed to develop their characters. We must not become like those individuals, or like the older son in the parable, nor like other biblical characters that had right conduct, but no character.

Jesus called the Pharisees whitewashed graves. He told them that they looked good on the outside, but on the inside, they were full of dead men's bones. We must avoid this at all costs.

Kingdom Notes:

The Dynamics of Discipleship

A Comprehensive Study of Discipleship and Service

The Dynamics of Discipleship
A Comprehensive Study of Discipleship and Service

-Section 3-

Keys to Kingdom Conduct

The Dynamics of Discipleship

A Comprehensive Study of Discipleship and Service

There are three things we must do to develop conduct fitting for the Kingdom of God. They are as follows:

1. Develop Kingdom Character

2. Deny the Flesh

3. Live by the Spirit, and

4. Obey the Word.

Kingdom Character

In our publication, "Let This Mind Be In You," we discussed Kingdom Character. It is the first key needed to have Kingdom Conduct. Without the character of Christ in you, you will not have the ability to deny the flesh and live by the Spirit.

Much of your good works will only come from vain motives. Having His nature enables you to have the proper conduct.

Deny the Flesh

Denial of the flesh is the second key to Kingdom Conduct. After striving daily to have His nature and character in us, we must then deny our flesh.

There are individuals whose characters are developing properly, but their actions are not reflecting the development. They have a heart and mind for God, but their fleshly desires still rule them.

We have debated for years about what Christians can and cannot do. The answer is simple. If your actions do not edify you or add to your spiritual life, you may want to abstain from them.

This may range from watching

certain television programs to being involved in particular conversations. We must remember the following exhortations of scripture:

> *All things are legitimate – permissible, and we are free to do anything we please; but not all things are helpful (expedient, profitable, and wholesome). All things are legitimate, but not all things are constructive to character] and edifying [to spiritual life].*

(I Corinthians 10:23 Amplified)

All unrighteousness is sin... (I John 5:17a)

Live by the Spirit

We then must live by the Spirit of God. Kingdom Conduct can only come as the result of yielding to the Spirit of God. We have two forces warring for control in our lives.

The flesh is in battle against the Spirit. Whichever of these have control in our lives will determine our behavior and conduct in the Kingdom.

How do we allow the Spirit of God to have control in our lives? We do this by living in the Spirit, sowing to the Spirit, and by crucifying the flesh through the Spirit.

If we live in the Spirit, we will be consumed with the desire for spiritual things. The more His presence is in our lives, the more we will desire it.

Christians also should sow to the Spirit. We sow to the Spirit, again, by praying, reading, and fellowship with other believers. This gives us the ability to crucify the lusts of the flesh.

Be not deceived; God is not mocked: for whatsoever a man soweth, that shall he also reap. For he that soweth to his flesh shall of the flesh reap corruption; but he that soweth to the Spirit shall of the Spirit reap life everlasting. (Galatians 6:7-8)

Obey the Word

The final key to Kingdom Conduct is obedience to the written

Word of God. Christians are accustomed to reading the Bible and hearing sermons, but many do not apply the information that is learned. Even if we are not mature, the Word of God is given to govern our actions as we move toward being perfect in Him. James told his readers that they must not only hear the Word, but also walk in it.

But be ye doers of the word, and not hearers only, deceiving your own selves. For if any be a hearer of the word, and not a doer, he is like unto a man beholding his natural face in a glass: For he beholdeth himself, and goeth his way, and straightway forgetteth what manner of man he was.(James 1:22-24)

Kingdom Notes:

The Dynamics of Discipleship

A Comprehensive Study of Discipleship and Service

-Section 4-

Rewards of Kingdom Conduct

God does not require us to abstain from evil to deny us pleasure or happiness. He does it so that He can pour out His blessings upon us. God tells us to be holy because He is holy.

When we have the right conduct, God cannot deny us our requests, except they be against His will. He will not withhold any good thing from those who walk upright before Him.

Because Hezekiah was a righteous man, God granted Him 15

more years to live. His obedience led to his reward. Our obedience will lead to God rewarding us. There are five major rewards to walking uprightly before the Lord.

They are healing, answered prayer, peace, long-life, and eternal life.

Healing

The first reward of Kingdom Conduct is healing. The Lord spoke to Solomon and told him that if His people would turn from their wicked ways that He would heal them. When we turn from our sins and weaknesses, God promises to heal us.

If my people, which are called by my name, shall humble themselves, and pray, and seek my face, and turn from their wicked ways; then will I hear from heaven, and will forgive their sin, and will heal their land. (II Chronicles 7:14)

Answered Prayer

Another reward for Kingdom

Conduct is answered prayer. God told us that if we abide in Him and follow His Word, we could ask for anything and He would do it.

How could He make such a promise? If we are abiding in the Word, we will only desire the will of God for our lives.

If ye abide in me, and my words abide in you, ye shall ask what ye will, and it shall be done unto you. (John 15:7)

Peace

Not only will God heal us and answer our prayers, but His peace will also be established in our lives.

Peace, I leave with you, my peace I give unto you; not as the world giveth, give I unto you. Let not your heart be troubled, neither let it be afraid. (John 14:27)

He also promises that He will bless us with long-life upon the face of the earth, if we would walk upright before Him.

He shall call upon me, and I will answer Him; I will be with him in trouble; I will deliver him. With long-life will I satisfy him, and show him my salvation. (Psalm 91:15-16)

Eternal Life

The greatest reward that God could bestow upon us for having Kingdom Conduct is eternal life. If we do not see the full manifestation of any of the other rewards, we can rest assured of this one. Because we believe in eternal life, we must have conduct appropriate for the Kingdom.

And every man that hath this hope (eternal life) in him purifieth himself, even as he is pure. (I John 3:3; Parenthesis mine)

These rewards come as a result of yielding to God and striving to walk according to His standards. Another final benefit of Kingdom Conduct is having the presence and power of God.

The Dynamics of Discipleship

A Comprehensive Study of Discipleship and Service

Kingdom Notes:

Bibliography

Evans, Roderick Levi (2018). The Development of the Disciple: The Preparation of the Christian for Ministry and Service. Abundant Truth Publishing: Camden, NC.

Evans, Roderick Levi (2024). Keys to Ministry: Discovering the Foundation for Service and Ministry in the Church. Abundant Truth Publishing: Camden, NC.

Evans, Roderick Levi (2024). Keys to the Promises of God: Maintaining Faith While You Wait. Abundant Truth Publishing: Camden, NC.

Evans Mister Roderick L. (2012). Walk in the Spirit: Biblical Studies in Christian Conduct. Abundant Truth Publishing: Camden, NC.

Kingdom Notes:

www.ingramcontent.com/pod-product-compliance
Lightning Source LLC
LaVergne TN
LVHW021655060526
838200LV00050B/2372